MARVEL IN MOTION

AND THE CHAOS UNDERNEATH

Mihaela-Adriana Bodea

BookLeaf Publishing

India | USA | UK

Web: www.bookleafpub.com

E-mail: info@bookleafpub.com

ISBN: 9789358360943

First edition 2021

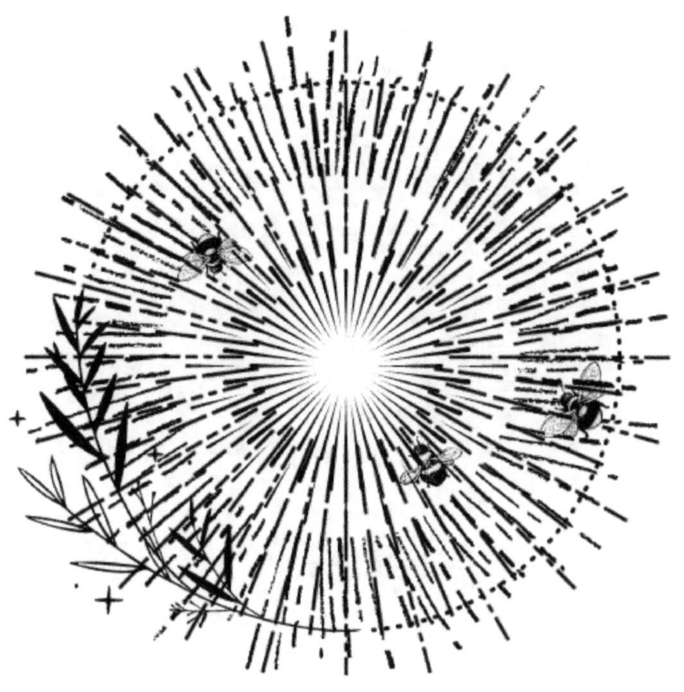

Preface

What is vulnerability?

I did not tell anyone I was writing this book. I was afraid that if I told someone, they would somehow take it away. A personal fear of mine.

Is this vulnerability? Me telling you this? … For me it's just a truth, one that I have to face, overcome and integrate. And why talk about something that is such a constant in one's life.

It is like marvelling at the weather in London.

Complaining about it won't change the fact…
So, I address my thoughts about the weather. I change
MY perspective about what the weather means.
Sometimes I take long walks and revel in it. Sometimes
I just want the weather to stop… And that I'm working
on it. And that I'm learning to trust the weather. I said
weather too many times. Weather, weather, weather.

So I decided not to tell anymore, but to show.

Yours Faithfully,
Weather

Acknowledgement

To all the past versions of who I was and what I am yet to become:

I'm so proud of all of you.

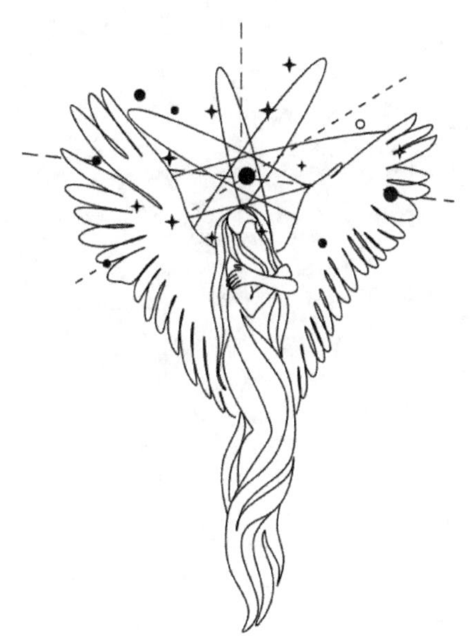

Dedication:

To Bia for her Resourcefulness,

To Chloe for her Realism,

To Lore for her Devotion,

To Maria for her Strength in Vision,

To Mishy for her Patience,

To Oana for her Generosity,

To Renata for her Optimism,

To Szido for her Practicality.

And to many other women and men who have been mirrors, showing me my fragmented self and thus helped me rebuild.

This book is dedicated to you.

Figure 1. This is us, exchanging ideas .I am taking the pic while Bia is on VideoCall because she decided to live in fucking Australia.

I. APPRECIATION

She coughs as she creaks,

I hear the words but she never speaks

An old **Bat** in a bag of bones

I hear goodbye as she floats on stones.

The softness of her steps

Could be that of ghosts.

It feels melodic, but I still cry the most.

Have you had your dinner, **Child**?

Yes. I scream into the wild.

Have you turned down the lamps, **Child**?

Yes. I wish my days away beguiled.

Have you read your future, **Child**?

No. There is no future. Only Now.

And as she nods her head along,

I see her head back down to **Avalon**.

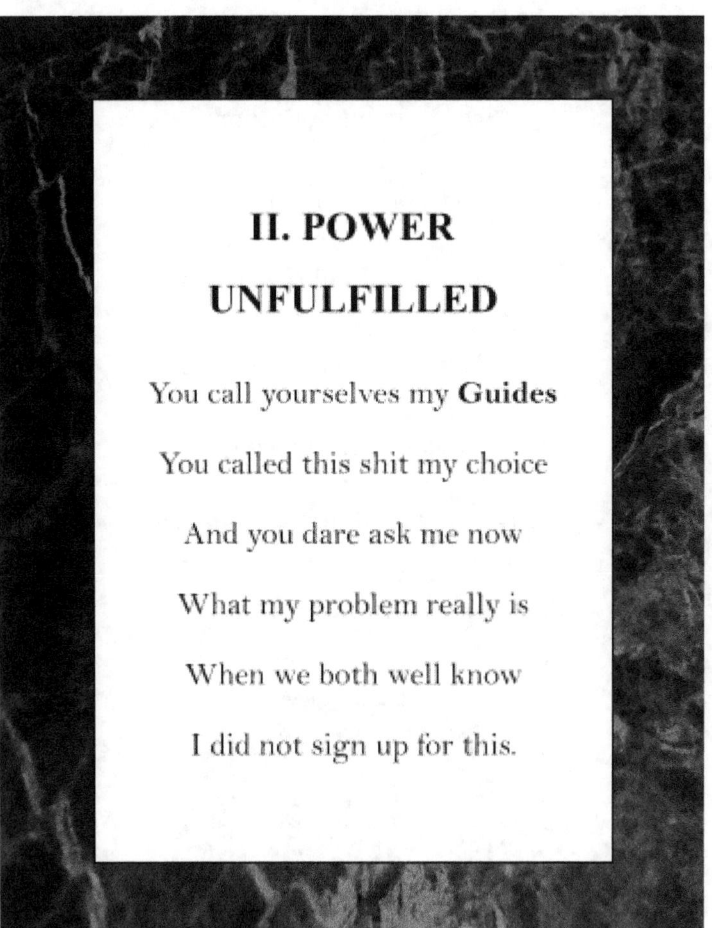

II. POWER
UNFULFILLED

You call yourselves my **Guides**

You called this shit my choice

And you dare ask me now

What my problem really is

When we both well know

I did not sign up for this.

You treat me like a newborn,

Every time I get reborn.

You erase my mind,

But leave behind my crimes.

And once I miss a step,

Once I fuck the **Help**

It's all downhill from there!

And you're the ones that get upset.

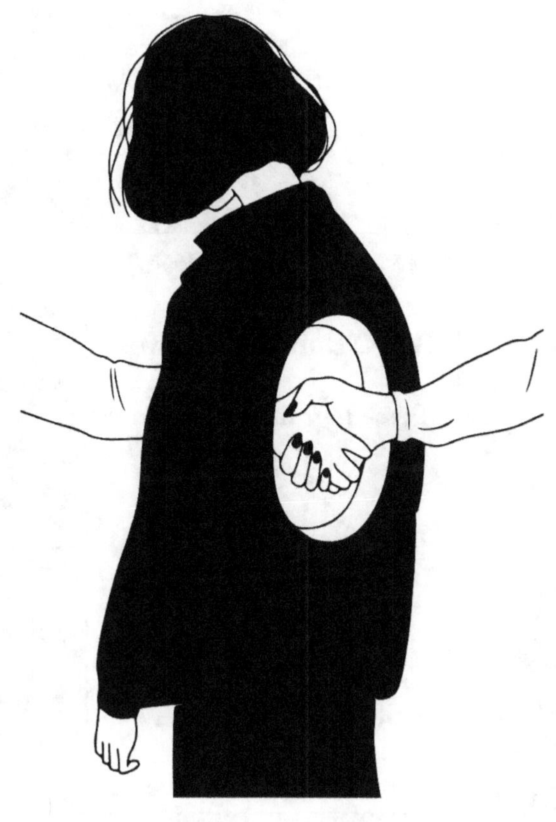

Does this sound even remotely correct?!?

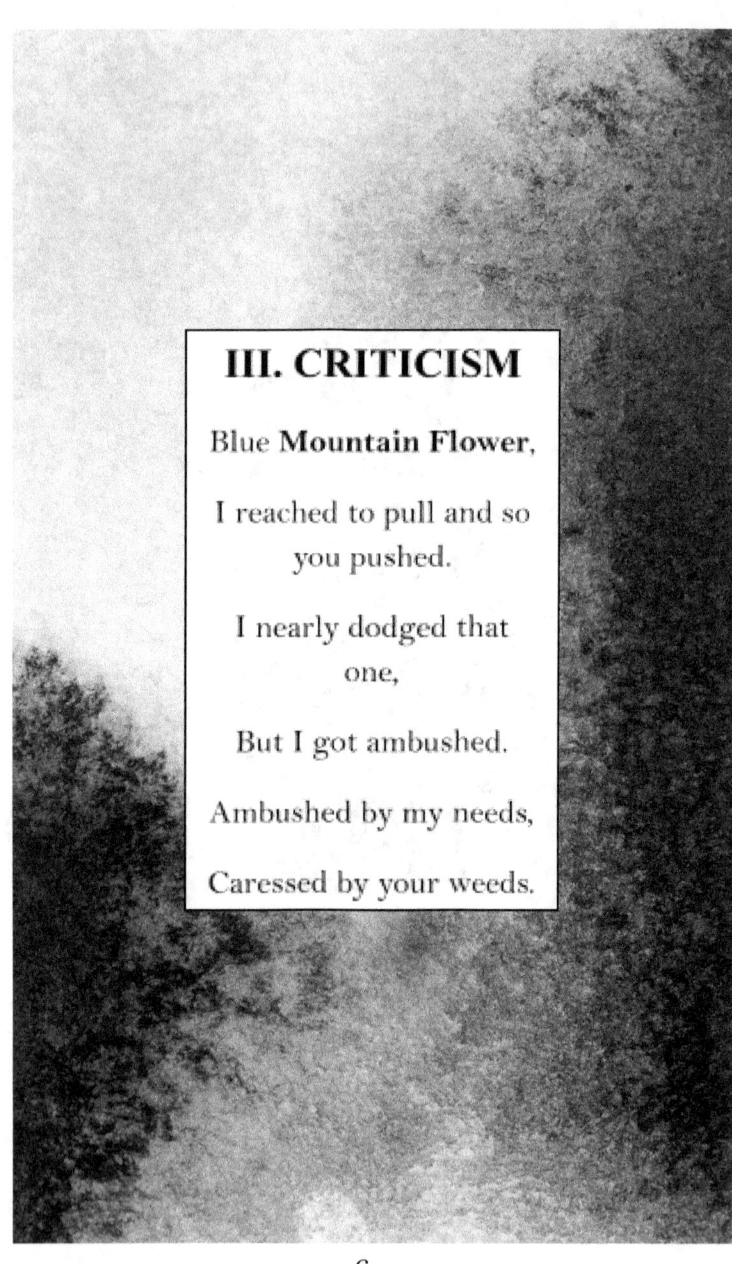

III. CRITICISM

Blue **Mountain Flower**,

I reached to pull and so
you pushed.

I nearly dodged that
one,

But I got ambushed.

Ambushed by my needs,

Caressed by your weeds.

Dear **Mountain Flower,**

I crossed a desert to get to
you

But in the end, all was
true.

All I got was **Sand**.

What was I expecting?

I know I was projecting.

IV. BLUFF

Jump,

The **Fool's** voice

whispers.

Jump, And you will see

How it was like,

What you were meant to be.

What was to happen

And why it never did…

Jump, the **Fool's** voice warns

Jump, and take the leap.

Do it for your youngsters!

Without you,

They'd be just monsters.

You cannot eat your own

But you can break them

Enough so that they never know

The true nature of their glow,

Not even for a second,

Not even for a minute.

You take that chance

And you just run with it.

Jump!

The **Fool** now thunders:

Jump, And you will see.

Come on, I dare
you

I dare you to be

Me.

V. ISOLATION

I look at you

Deep in your sleep,

And wonder

Where do you go

In your dreams?

What do you do?

I see your eyes flutter,

And I want to interject

Can I just bother

You with some regrets?

Do you swim around in Creation?

Marvel at the vast Nations?

Look around at hierarchies

And mask your veiled mutations

In a world of sheer negotiations?

Or do you marvel back at **Stars**,

While you're pushed around in cars

And you feel that you are broken

But you don't let that shit in

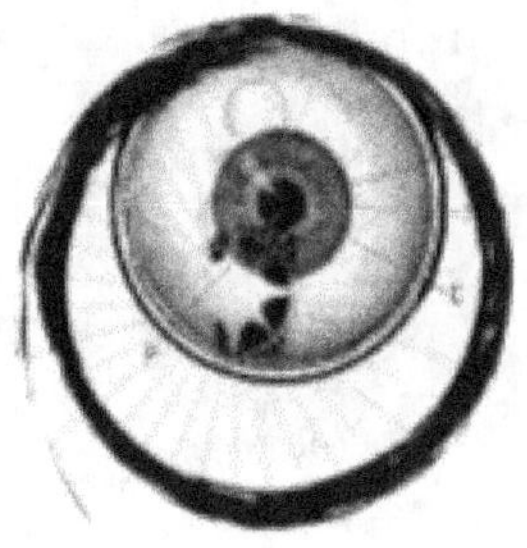

Cause you've always felt so numb

While the world just calls you dumb

But you're strong, you don't succumb.

And as you look back at the

start,

As you look back on **Creation**

Through the eyes of a

Manifestation

You can't help but wonder in

elation

Is this supposed to be a

Vacation?

VI. Enterprise

People say **Hell** is ablaze

With the sins of mankind,

But I know for a fact

Fire is a sign of loving.

And **Love** walks both the
Earth

And the **Heavens**.

VII. CHAOS ALONE

Love, the children keep growing

The leaves on trees keep falling

And I'm still here.

I see the seasons change

Slowing down the pace

And I'm still here.

I wonder if you even hear me...

And all I keep thinking is

If I don't push the brakes today

Loneliness might go away,

Promise me you'll meet me

Maybe just halfway?

VIII. CHAOS & ORDER

For now, please look away.

I can't stand the thought

Of you seeing me this way.

What have I become?

Where will I still go?

Why did you have to leave?

I would have loved to see you grow.

I can't even say **Hello.**

It's such a shame

God stopped your glow.

But don't you worry, I won't go.

I still have the life I know

But I miss the shit out of you so

Keep a seat for me

Way down below.

And when I'm ready,

We'll run the show.

I promise you, We won't lay low

But for now, Don't wait for me

Go on just, **Grow**.

IX. EGOTISM

I hear a voice , deep in the
woods

But I walk away confused...

"I was already an old man
when I was born

I was stripped away, never
to mourn…

Mourn the children, mourn
my wife

As they took away my knife.

Mourn all merits, mourn all
wolves,

Mourn the blood on these
thick shoes.

And yet, you don't hear

me complaining!

Get up and move

Stop over explaining!"

X. VISION

I hear the knock

(It grows louder)

As I turn towards the **Clock**

(A dark night, no power.)

The **Moon** guides my eyes

(Feel how it endows her.)

To the **Light** at the entrance

(Letting the silence all devour).

I heard you came back

(I feel somehow empowered).

Oh, to see your face again

(Gentle, a **Flower**)

You're here, I whisper

(He'll be gone within the hour)

I start my slow walk

(Down the ladder of a **Tower**)

Down some steep steps

(Brisk, as I cower)

While my stomach turns to slush

(I wish for a rain, a shower)

Can you forgive my calling?

(I look and I wonder)

Will you be **Happy** here?

(Cause I often feel overpowered)

XI. PROTECTION

You know those sneaky

little things,

The ones that sleep behind

an ear

Or hide under the eye?

The ones that puncture

wings

And bring down **Kings**?

They sneak in at **Night**,

Make beds in **Minds**, then

bite.

The kind that live

In hard to reach places

Dark and damp,

Along the breaches.

Gaps in your wellbeing,

Breaks in your defences.

I saw one today

And asked it what it
teaches.

I knew it came to stay,

Its hand far reaches.

Ripe and plum,

It looked askew

Like a toddler with the flu.

I initiate a sort of dialogue

Primitive in nature,

I treat it as a dog

Didn't want to scare the

being

I threw it a blanket of light,

For its own wellbeing.

I must've known

It would be fleeing

Before I even got a chance to yell

Behind his flee, he left a smell

A smell of **Fear**, a sign to foretell

It's ever growing presence

Behind an **Eye**, under the nose

Right behind your inner sigh.

But alas, it ran away

Before I could even say:

"See you next time

You tried your way!

Don't you fret

I know you've gone astray.

You've been feeding off others

Trying to obey

Your incessant need to find a prey.

I'll be waiting,

Be prepared

I'm so done playing

You've had your share."

XII. REBELLION

As I re-read this whole thing,

As I look at editing,

As I strip away false control

On some thing that took its toll

I just keep remembering

Lust and love are two whole things

Individually arrest,

Hungry at their breast,

Lonesome in their nest,

Wholesome when they're blessed.

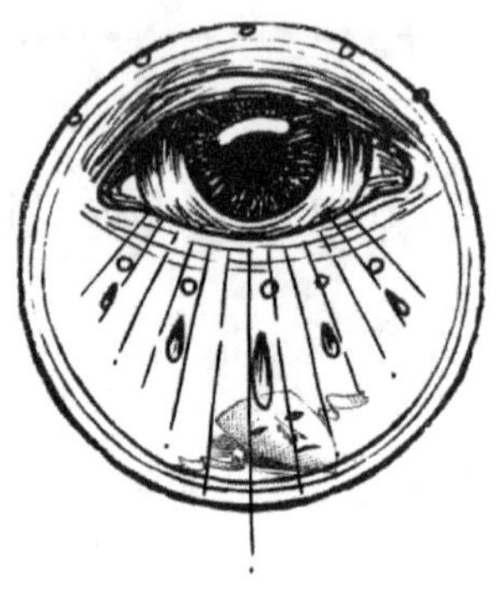

Love, my dear just smile

Lust, my love- denial

Why do we become so hostile?

Is there a way out of control

While unshackling

Our individual parole.

XIII. SELF-DEFENCE

Skipping down a flight of stairs

Skip around table and chairs

Carpets and drapes,

Long sheets falling

I hear nearby,

My **Grand Mother** calling.

She pulls at curtains

And shouts through walls.

And I have ears to **See** them all.

Down the road, behind the **Wall**.

In the cemetery, there's always a
brawl.

I walk along the **Riverside**

The shallow sides are deep and wide

The **Dead Men** rise without failing

As I hear the **Mermen** wailing.

All of these sounds in my ears,

And all I can think of is my tears.

I walk along the narrow path

Too frightened and scared

To take the Bath

And as I wish upon

The fateful **Stars,**

I stopped thinking

About my scars

While I yell

Into the **Dark** that's set

To never

Let me, ever forget

(Still I feel

My insides crawling)

The sound of my lovely

Grand Mother calling.

XIV. INTUITION

The **Sun** ,scorching

Gave the grave-diggers

A well-deserved
warning.

They usually happily
feast

Unaware of their
presence

At the **Goddess's** teat.

An army of archaeologists

Labour intently at its
entrance

Where my **Heart**, unused
lies

And my **Mind** will not
assist

Another day in the **Abyss**.

But the **Fool** inside me
screams:

"The **Love** I know will
find me,

I will use this as my
plea

And you will all bear
witness

To the **Love** that has
followed me.

From **Nothingness** to
the **Abyss,**

I will set myself **Free**

Because The day I met
you,

Heaven crashed into
me.

ALL XV.   **RICHES**

"The **Abyss** smiles back:

Good girl."

XVI. ACQUISITION

"Can I go **Home** now? " – I fly by

Staring into the volcano's eye.

I pace along, not sure if the now-

Would be the best time to

Kick a pebble into its bowel-

I try my **Luck** and close my **Eye**

Nothing, confused
replies:

Have you no questions
about your ailments? "

My body relaxes and
mind gets clearer

As I realise the
Darkness has not
looked inside my mirror

(Good, nothing mentioned

About my derailments…

Like how I sabotaged myself,

Or how I put myself on a shelf

Mute and quiet cause I do not know

What it is I need deep down below,

Soooo…

I just sit and whisper things

Into the **Quiet**,

Where **Truth** usually sings.)

"I assume I'll find out along the way."

I say right back as I just wanna go away...

"Ok human, go."

Nothingness reads my mind.

"See you next time,"

I say and go to sign.

"See you soon,"

Nothingness reaches to the **Divine**.

(All in all, I think that went great.)

I say to myself

With a lil bit of hate.

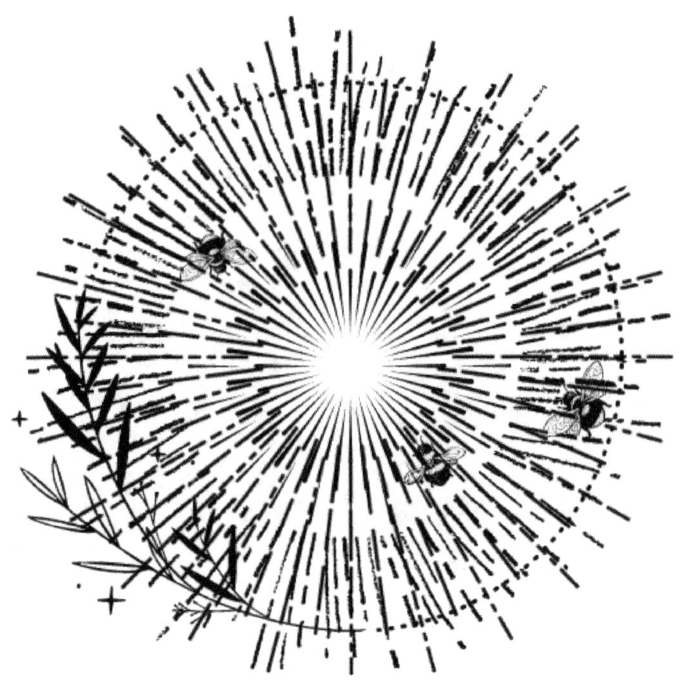

XVII. PRINCIPLE

Walking back from my

Trial

I stare back, half in
denial

What I did, what I will
do

Will it be enough just
for the two?

For my mother, for my
father

For the children I will
bother?

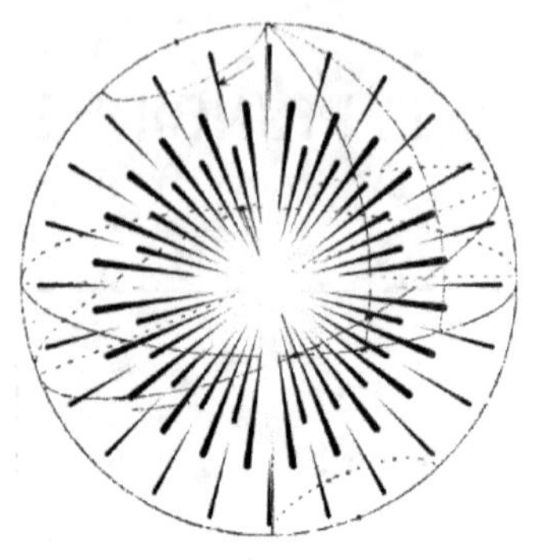

Bring them up

And keep them close

I can hear whispers of **Angels** notes:

"It seems you have forgotten

What you're here to do,

You won't do more

Cosmic order you won't restore.

If you do decide

To go against your tide

The **Order** will let it slide

In the eyes of **Source**

You'll remain a **Bride**.

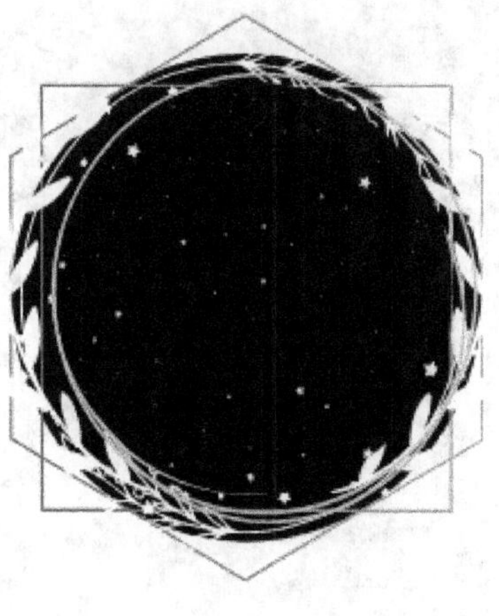

Or you could do

More

For your father,

For your mother,

For your children,

While you continue

To smother,

Smother the **Life**

Out of another.

And never realise

The **Truth**

Behind your real bother.

Or you could take the life

Which has been given

And forge the **Path**

That will have risen.

You are driven to uphold

Such graceful command,

Just take the hold…

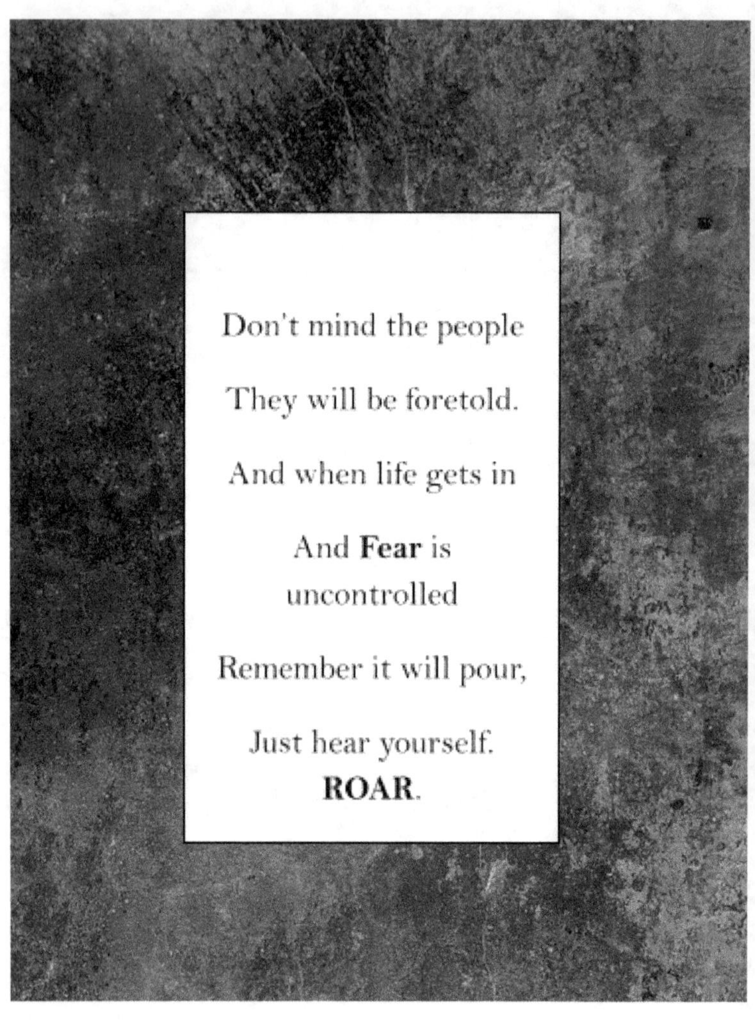

Don't mind the people

They will be foretold.

And when life gets in

And **Fear** is
uncontrolled

Remember it will pour,

Just hear yourself.
ROAR.

XVIII. POWER

Thank you to all the poems

that have not made it

into the final product.

I acknowledge you.

But not all things are meant for you.

XIX. DISCOVERY

I remember myself

Running out of a forest

Out of a reality I could not forget

But dared not accept.

Although the Gods cautioned

I misdirected my gaze

And looked back towards that clock

As I begged its hands to stop.

Stop for the night,

Stop for the evening,

Stop this endless feeling

For I can't face its meaning.

Let me rest my head

Near this lover of mine

That seems to follow me

Every time I try to climb.

XX. ECCENTRICITY

Once I was a **Goddess**

Now I am a **Man**.

Dressed in turnip red

Fearing where I stand.

Once I was a **Goddess**

Now I am a **Woman**

But that didn't last long.

I was taken by the hand

Led into a field

Across the whole
expand,

I even crossed a line

But all I ever found was
Sand

Mere crumbs of waste
and blood

At my killers feet I
stand,

Unmanned.

Once I was a **Goddess**

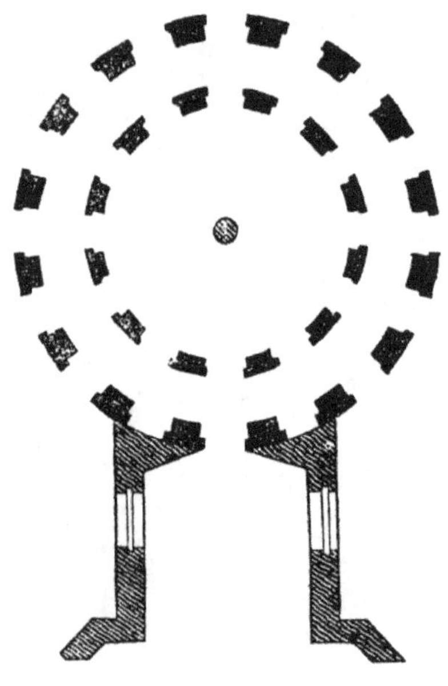

Now I am a **Man**.

Deep inside a war raged on.

But I can see I have no plan

Once I was a **Goddess**…

And now I fear the **Madman**.

XXI. DETACHMENT

What is there to do

When the real problem

Wasn't even you?

What is there to learn

When the worst

Made a return

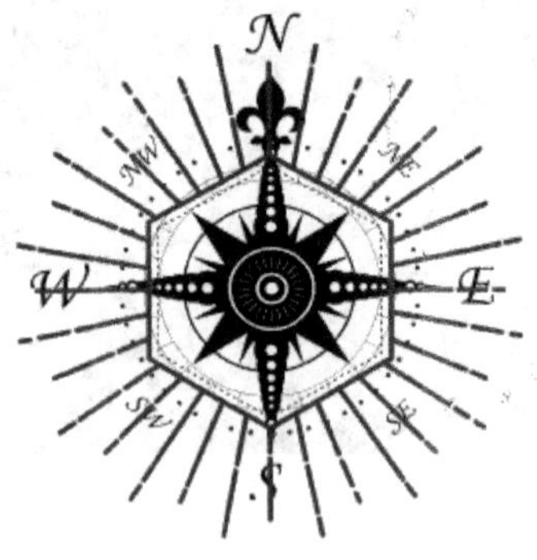

What is there to do

When that which wasn't real

Turned true?

XXII. SUBMISSION

What is it that I own or do

That you so easily break in two

As you make me go through

What I don't want to!

Don't just stand there!

See all of my **Glory**

Don't just cats away part of my **Story**

Wish me well or stand in line,

Cause I've seemed to have lost my
spine

And now I come to you to purge

As I undress my deep filled urge

To smother you

Head to toe, in warm **Taboo**.

I walk along the river

(I feel I have to be a giver)

Down to a place I once knew

Where once, we were the two

And as I lay down

To kiss the waters,

You tell me you're not in the mood

But you still want me to show you
gratitude.

(What a fucking prude.)

The XXIIIrd Choice

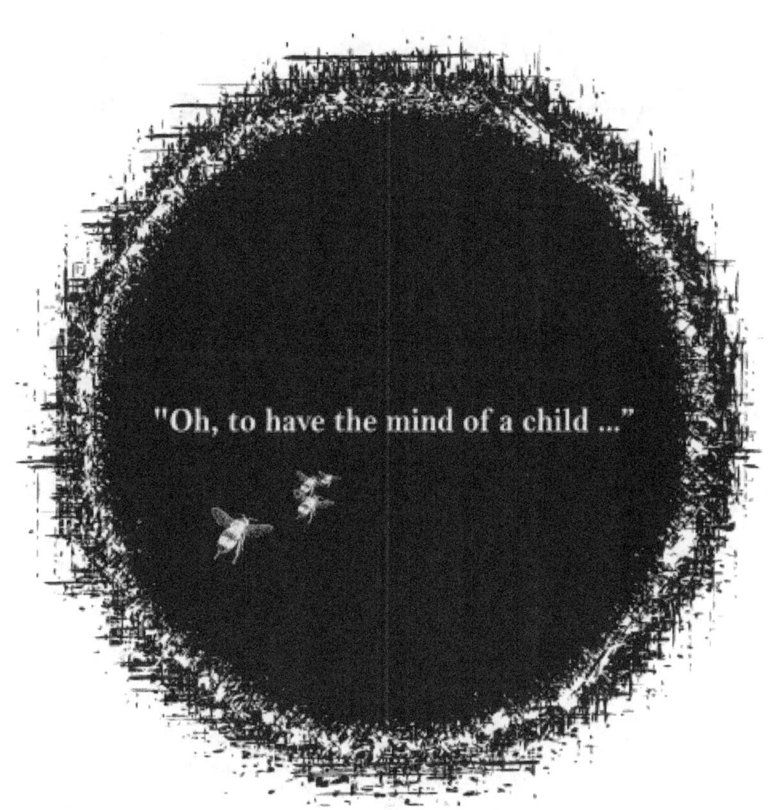

I hear them whisper as I stroll back down the **Mountain**.

They wish me well and grant me passage

And as I find myself again, at the end of the **World**,

I can't help but **Smile**.